THE AMERICAN SCHEME

Volume One:
An Insider's Look at Poverty in America

Jared A. Snyder

SYNESI PUBLISHING
Buffalo, Wyoming

Library of Congress Control Number: 2017917791

Published by:

Synesi Publishing (An imprint of Zoe's Publishing)

Zoe's Publishing, LC
412 N. Main Street
Suite 100
Buffalo, Wyoming

zoespublishing.com
synesipublishing.com

Printed in the United States of America

First Printing, 2017

ISBN 978-0-9993926-3-8

"The world is a dangerous place, not because of those who do evil, but because of those who look on and do nothing."

- Albert Einstein

CONTENTS

PREFACE

The American Scheme series offers a look at some of the most prominent problems in the United States today. Its volumes are not intended to be manifests of hatred toward the nation, but merely guides written to shine a light on common issues that plague every nation in the world. So why write guides specifically tailored to expose these issues in America? For many decades, it has been referred to as a land of opportunity, of milk and honey, of freedom. However, those phrases are misleading marketing slogans that came about during a major period of immigration in America, between 1870 and 1900. It's not to say that those things don't exist in America, but they surely are not proprietary or genuine to the country, nor are they as freely and widely available as many people around the world are led to believe. This series focuses on offering its readers, whether near or far, a look at life in America for the average person, one which isn't embellished with marketing slogans or other devices of nationalism.

Your tour guide for these close-up views of life in the United States is none other than series author Jared A. Snyder. Highly qualified to speak on all of the subject matter covered in The American Scheme series, his firsthand experiences with poverty, homelessness, hunger, and numerous other aspects of American life offer a unique perspective. He is a man of great faith who believes that people should be prioritized over nationalistic *blah-blah* (or patriotism as it's referred to in the USA). So, come along with Jared as he paints a vivid picture of what it's really like living in America for an average individual. Throughout the course of this book, and the series, you will read firsthand accounts detailing how the same issues that plague other nations plague the USA as well. Hopefully, you will gather insight you haven't gotten elsewhere by reading this series. The American Scheme series is truly an insider's look into how life in the United States of America can really be.

INTRODUCTION

What Is Poverty

Before understanding the magnitude at which poverty effects America, we must first come to an understanding of what I mean when I say the term, poverty. What is it? According to Merriam-Webster's online dictionary, poverty is, "The state of one who lacks a usual or socially acceptable amount of money or material possessions." So just considering the dictionary definition alone, we see that the word poverty possesses a lot of grey area in that it mentions a "usual or socially acceptable amount." That amount will, obviously, be relative to the economic conditions of the society to which the word is being applied. That means poverty in a third-world country and a first-world country (such as America) will look notably different, but in both cases, it is poverty nonetheless. Unfortunately, you probably haven't thought of poverty like that up till now, because the typical images of poverty that we're exposed to, the ones that have been burned into our brains, are those of third-world countries. Then again, perhaps you live in one of the third-world countries, and so your understanding of poverty is going to differ from someone who lives in a first-world country. In either circumstance, we must come to an agreement that poverty is poverty, whether it plagues a first-world or third-world country. In this guide, we will be considering poverty relative to the United States of America, a first-world country.

Still, we need to establish a more concrete definition of the term, since it looks different depending on the economic conditions of the society it's being applied to. The United States of America is made up of 50 individual states, and numerous territories as well. Regardless, the economic conditions of the nation can and do vary from those of an individual state, and the economic conditions from state to state tend to vary as well. But we're supposed to be narrowing things down to create a finite understanding of the term poverty. Okay, I have to confess, I've been overdoing this "finite definition" thing a bit to illustrate a point. There is no finite definition of the word poverty. In an August 22, 2017, article appearing on Forbes' website, contributor Chuck DeVore poses a brilliant question, "Why do two government poverty yardsticks generate very different results?" He goes on to explain that there is no common benchmark by which to measure poverty with and that the measure currently being used is fairly antiquated. It is based on a food consumption survey from the US Department of Agriculture that originated more than 60 years ago. That survey was created to determine the cost of a subsistence diet. However, in order to measure poverty, the results of that survey are simply multiplied by three.

So, according to the research conducted by Mr. DeVore, we cannot finitely define the term poverty, and moreover, the benchmark used by the US Federal Government is quite antiquated and probably doesn't accurately represent the extent to which poverty plagues America. Instead, we are given an "averaged weighted" figure, as the US Census Bureau puts it, which leads one to believe that things are much better than they probably are. That's not to say that things in America aren't decent, aren't sustainable, but they are not as glorious as the American establishment would have you believe.

All across America, there are those who are struggling to keep a roof over their head; over their family's heads. There are those who are struggling to keep food on the table, and to keep the heat running during the cold winter months. In urban areas, there are many people who depend on public transit, and not because they enjoy waiting for long periods of time out in the elements, but because they are unable to afford to purchase a vehicle of their own. Just look at the number of homeless people living on the streets in major cities like Los Angeles, Chicago, and New York, and you will surely begin to form a better understanding of what poverty in America really looks like, as opposed to the image the establishment is trying to paint of a land that is greatly flourishing. America is referred to as the "land of opportunity," but there are more people living here who won't ever fully experience that sentiment than will. I, for one, am an American who has been plagued by poverty, and I aim to share those experiences with you in order to help you understand what poverty looks like for an American.

An Insider's Look at Poverty in America

In chapter one, I will elaborate on my background as an impoverished American. For the record, I have almost a decade of experience living in poverty in my adult life. During my childhood, my family endured periods of poverty as well. So, I guess you might say I am a poverty expert, which is actually something nobody should have to profess. As I write this guide, I am still living in poverty. That said, I'm also very blessed. Although I am homeless, I have a roof over my head. I also have some experience living on the streets too. I can also count my blessings in that I have food to eat each day, which has not always been the case. I sincerely know what it means to be hungry, malnourished even. Those times were extremely rough. I lost dangerous amounts of weight and experienced other side effects as well. And while it might seem like I'm trying to play the victim card here, nothing could be further from the truth. I am working diligently to turn my life around, but as a new author, I am faced with the challenge of proving myself as an expert on the topics that I write about. So, I share with you the honest reasons why I consider myself an expert on the topic of poverty in America and hope that you will agree that I am, in fact, qualified to speak on the topic.

Poverty Statistics for The Land of Opportunity

After sharing my own experiences with poverty, we will consider poverty statistics for the "Land of Opportunity." While I do not believe that you will question my ability to speak on the topic of poverty in America, after reading of my firsthand experiences with it, it would be arrogant of me to assume that my experiences alone create a sufficient representation of its reach. After all, one man's experiences are just that, his experiences. However, the whole reason I'm writing this guide is to shed light on poverty's vast reach in America, which is commonly overlooked because of things like nationalism being paraded about as patriotism. Now, I am certain that some of my readers are grumbling at that comment because they are, in fact, the faux patriots I am speaking of and believe that I just demonstrated a level of hatred for America. That is not true. Before I go on, I want to take a moment to explain the commonly misunderstood difference between patriotism and nationalism, which will clarify why I've indicated it as a reason for the lack of recognition of poverty's presence in America.

To save on time, I am going to defer explaining the difference between patriotism and nationalism to the late Sydney J. Harris, an American journalist who wrote for the Chicago Daily News, and then later for the Chicago Sun-Times. In one of his articles, he is said to have written the following:

Patriotism is proud of a country's virtues and eager to correct its deficiencies; it also acknowledges the legitimate patriotism of other countries, with their own specific virtues. The pride of nationalism, however, trumpets its country's virtues and denies its deficiencies, while it is contemptuous toward the virtues of other countries. It wants to be, and proclaims itself to be, "the greatest," but greatness is not required of a country; only goodness is.

So, you see, there is a distinct difference between the two terms, even though they are commonly used synonymously. And though you might argue that it's not a big deal, it is. In his essay, Notes on Nationalism, George Orwell comments on the importance of distinguishing between the two terms: "Nationalism is not to be confused with patriotism. Both words are normally used in so vague a way that any definition is liable to be challenged, but one must draw a distinction between them, since two different and even opposing ideas are involved."

If the extra time I've taken hasn't clarified things for the naysayers by now, nothing will. However, this is not a book about the difference between nationalism and patriotism, but one about the issue of poverty in America. Though I will argue wholeheartedly that its lack of attention is largely due to nationalism being passed off as patriotism, my digression must end here.

Commentary and Solutions

Finally, in chapter 3, I will wrap up volume one of this series by providing my own commentary on the topic at hand, as well as providing some ideas in terms of solutions that I believe could make a big impact. As you might have guessed by now, I will spend more time on the assertion that nationalism is largely to blame for the lack of recognition of poverty in America. However, it is not the only issue hindering more people from understanding the extent to which poverty affects the nation. There are other issues that are contributing, both, to the festering of poverty and its lack of attention by Americans, and by the rest of the world for that matter. Over the course of the chapter, I will outline some of these other contributing factors and provide insight as to where they stem from. And because I am of the belief that one should have solutions ready to share after airing their grievances, I will spend the remainder of the chapter going over several solutions I feel could realistically make a positive impact on the issue of poverty in America. Not only that but also on effectively rephrasing the American narrative in order to properly reflect its strengths and its weaknesses. You may find yourself in total disagreement with what I have to say, but remember, I am speaking as someone who has a lot of firsthand experience with poverty as an American. I have lived with and have evaluated these conditions for almost a decade now. Ergo, the commentary and solutions I provide regarding poverty, and especially poverty in America, are coming from a true insider.

CHAPTER ONE
An Insider's Look at Poverty in America

This Is Poverty

If you didn't over-ambitiously skip over the introduction to get to this chapter, then you'll recall that we determined there is no finite way to define poverty. If you did skip the introduction, I suggest you go back and read it so that this chapter and those that follow make sense, in terms of purpose and placement. As there is no way to finitely define the term poverty, this chapter exists to paint a picture of what it looks like in America. Furthermore, as I also indicated in the introduction, this chapter exists to establish my credibility to speak as an expert on the topic of poverty in America.

It's hard to believe that something as awful as poverty lacks a finite definition, especially with how widespread it is throughout the world. Then again, it also makes sense that there is no finite definition because, as we've learned, what poverty is and looks like varies greatly from place to place, and is dependent upon the social and economic conditions of the area or society that it plagues. So, what poverty looks like in America will vary from what poverty looks like in, let's say, Romania. That's because social and economic conditions between America and Romania also vary. Now, in case you've forgotten, let's consider again what is meant when I refer to the social and economic conditions of a place that is affected by poverty. While attempting to define poverty in the introduction, we considered the definition provided by Merriam-Webster's online dictionary. It indicates that poverty is a lack of "a usual or socially acceptable amount of money or material possessions." And, as we can deduce on our own, that amount of money or material possessions is dependent upon the society or place being considered. While I cannot speak authoritatively on what poverty looks like in a place like Romania, I can speak quite confidently on what poverty looks like in America. After all, that is the place where I live and the society that I am part of.

I suspect that there are some of you who might believe that poverty is something a child couldn't possibly understand. Let me assure you that the children living in poverty are quite aware of it and the suffering that it causes. As a child, I can vividly remember what poverty looked like for my family. Before I get too far ahead, let me fill you in on some details regarding my family. I am the second youngest of eight kids, all from the same parents. We lived in a three-story house that had four bedrooms and one bathroom. My father was eventually able to afford to complete the second bathroom on the third floor, but that wasn't until my mid-teen years. As a child, 10 people shared one bathroom. Ironically enough, the house always seemed a lot bigger to us kids. And in all honesty, it actually worked out a lot better than you might suspect it would for a family as large as mine. My father worked very hard to earn enough to support us while my mother faithfully stayed at home each day to care for us. At one point in time, my father was working two full-time jobs to support us and we still needed food stamps.

Speaking of food, when you're living in poverty you have fewer choices in terms of food variety. You simply buy what you can afford, and in our case, there were a lot of mouths to feed. I can remember my mom going through a bean phase. I cannot tell you how many ways I've had beans prepared, and all different types at that. At that time, they were what we could afford, so they're what we ate. And as much as my siblings and I groaned, we were thankful for them. In addition to beans, there was a chicken phase too. Despite having a very tight budget, my parents did their best to make sure we were eating healthy. There are some people living in poverty who are not fortunate enough to say that. We scarcely ate out at restaurants because my father would have had to take a third full-time job to afford it. For a child, though, it was hard for me to hear friends talking about cool restaurants they went to because I felt uncool, like an outsider. Admittedly, as an adult, I look back and think how silly it was of me, but as a child in grade school, it was more important to fit in and feel socially accepted. And although there were two people working hard to make sure that us kids never went hungry, that wasn't the case for me as an adult. I've gone to bed hungry many nights, sometimes only having one small meal during the day and other times having nothing to eat at all. It all depended on how much I was able to earn any given day, and sometimes that was nothing. I'm certain you've heard of people living "paycheck-to-paycheck." I was living day-to-day, scrambling to find work. I will touch on this more in the next section, but I wanted to create a comparison between food availability when I was a child in poverty to food availability when I was an adult in poverty.

Moving along from food, I want to talk about material possessions. As a devout man of God, large amounts of fancy material possessions are not all that important to me. However, as human beings, we require a minimum amount of material possessions to live. I'm talking about things like clothes, shoes, hygiene products, and other essentials. As you might suspect, I have a lot of experience with hand-me-downs. In fact, the only things that weren't handed down were socks, underwear, and shoes. Although, winter boots were. Yes, I was certainly glad to have clothes to wear, but again, there is a very heavy emphasis on fitting in when you're a child in school. When money was really tight, worn out hand-me-downs were mended and patched. I look at photos from when I was a kid and get a chuckle out of seeing myself in clothes that didn't quite fit right. That's because a lot of the hand-me-downs were hand-me-downs. There were families at our church who would send over bags of used clothes, which was incredibly nice of them but things didn't always fit right. One of the perks, though, was that sometimes there would be a brand-name garment or two. Not that brand name is all that important, but for a kid who just wants to fit in, it certainly helps in their mind. And since there was no way of knowing when the next bag of clothes would be coming, we wore things until they couldn't possibly be worn anymore, and that includes shoes. I've had pairs of shoes that were so worn out, they looked like they were singing a chorus each time I took a step because the soles had separated from the body of the shoe.

As an adult living in poverty, things aren't quite the same. There is nobody else making sure I can get dressed every day, it's totally up to me. I've learned the importance of taking extra good care of the clothes I do have, and when somebody wants to buy me a gift for my birthday or Christmas, I have no problem asking for clothes if I need them. That's something I would have never asked for as a kid. Another difference is that, as a kid, I had no problem getting rid of old clothes for replacements. As an adult, even when I get new or replacement clothes, I am not as hasty to get rid of the old. I don't have many possessions. In fact, the sum of what I own fits easily into a Toyota Corolla. However, the majority of those possessions are clothing; at least 90%. There are some good reasons why I do as I do when it comes to clothing. For one thing, dressing nicer gives me an upper hand when it comes to finding decent work. For another thing, living in a wealthy city in Southern California, dressing nicer keeps the police from stopping me every time they see me walking down the sidewalk. Though I've since moved on, the city I lived in for nearly 10 years has a reputation for not taking kindly to anyone who doesn't "look like they belong." Homeless people are said to be shipped out of the city. I'm not absolutely sure if that is true or not, but I've only seen a homeless person sleeping on a bus bunch there once, and there was a police officer helping him collect his things.

In America, people living in poverty and the homeless are often looked down upon, as if they are less than human. In my best estimation, most people who are better off think of the less fortunate types as being drug addicts, drunkards, or deadbeats. A lot of people have asked me over the years, "Why don't you just get a job?" Unfortunately, it's not as easy for me to get a job as it might be for the person asking the question. I have a story, just like everybody else, and there are reasons why I cannot simply go and "get a job." Moreover, it's not that I haven't tried getting sustaining work, nor continue to try. I am forced to accept work within certain parameters because of my personal situation. I wrote a memoir titled, Dear Baby: Letters To A Child Who Was Never Mine which explains my unique situation in great detail. The consequences I outline in the book are the reason why I am forced to live in poverty, and also why it is so hard for me to get sustaining employment. Yet I, like other unfortunate individuals, commonly get categorized as a lazy deadbeat. It is largely why I have avoided using any sort of public services as much as possible, so that presumptuous Zounderkites don't have anything over me. Though, I have had to depend on public services a time or two, and I'll discuss that in the next section.

Abject Poverty: Lower Than Poverty

You might be of the understanding that poverty is poverty. It is a terrible circumstance of life that many are faced with across the world. You would be correct in asserting that poverty is terrible and that there are many people across the world whose lives are plagued by it, but poverty is not simply poverty. There actually exists a far worse type of poverty, abject poverty. Now, I'll be the first to admit that the poverty I experienced as a child is nowhere near as bad as it is for other children in America, and the poverty that I experience as a child is not even comparable to the poverty I've experienced as an adult. Abject poverty is most simply understood as being poverty that is much more extreme than poverty. Those living in abject poverty make the otherwise impoverished grateful not to be in the same situation. And, as an adult, abject poverty has plagued my life far worse than poverty ever plagued my childhood.

In my adult life, there have only been two times when I've afforded to keep a roof over my head. Once was when I rented a room from a Chinese family. It cost me $650 per month, and

I struggled and scrambled just to be able to earn that amount each month, which often resulted in me having to choose between buying groceries, keeping a roof over my head, or keeping my cell phone on. All three of those things are important. There was one other time when I shared an apartment with a guy in Sherman Oaks, California. I had to sell a bunch of photo and video equipment I had to afford that place, which only lasted a few months and removed the possibility of me getting photo and video related work. It turned out that my roommate was squandering the rent money on partying with his friends, so we ended up getting evicted from that place. I no sooner got settled in and was faced with trying to find somewhere else to go. Aside from those two instances, I have spent my adult life as a couch surfer, mostly sleeping on couches, floors, and even in a recliner chair. A time or two, a spare bedroom with a comfy bed made me feel like a normal human being. Otherwise, I slept wherever there was a space available. Anything was better than having to sleep on the street, which I have a little experience with as well. You might be surprised with how comfortable a sleeping bag on a hardwood floor actually is when you're homeless. Worrying about where I would sleep at night was never even a thought when I was a child. However, it is something that is regularly on my mind as an adult. Many people have suggested that I find some sort of housing program that could help me but, unfortunately, there aren't too many programs available for single, healthy, adult males. The few that do exist have waiting lists a mile long. Yes, there are shelters available, but I can't fall asleep in unfamiliar surroundings with strangers. Furthermore, most shelters operate on a first come-first served basis, so you have to wait in line all day. If I'm waiting in line all day, then that means I am not out looking for work to help elevate my situation. It's a paradox, really.

As I had mentioned in the previous section, there has been a time or two when I've had to use public services. They were food stamps and health care. I honestly tried to avoid using them at all costs, because pride told me that I should. Also, I didn't want to face scrutiny from others. In terms of healthcare, I was forced to enroll in the public health program by Obamacare mandates that required everyone to carry health insurance. However, in terms of food stamps, that was a choice I made after wrestling with my pride (and hunger) for some time. My "other mom" sat me down and explained to me that I had paid income taxes for a number of years and that I should be able to use such a program now that I needed it.

"That's what they're there for," she concluded. In all honesty, it had gotten pretty bad for me. At one point in time, it had gotten to the point where I'd have to wake up before the sun and make a visit to all of the nearby garbage dumpsters and cans, searching for bottles and cans I could return for the deposit money. The caveat is that I wasn't the only person doing that, so I had to be very swift about it. Some days there were enough for me to buy a little bit of food, but other times there was nothing, and I'd then resort to looking for some sort of odd job on Craigslist. I also ended up having to sell anything of value that I owned. For a time, right before I broke down and decided to apply for food stamps, I went through a potato phase. All I could afford were potatoes, so that's what I bought. I'd fry them up, and sometimes I'd manage to also afford some vegetables or hot dogs to throw into the mix. A time or two, I even managed to afford a small amount of cheese. As sick as I was getting of potatoes, I would have happily kept eating them just to sustain myself because there was a time when I couldn't even afford them. There was a time when I'd go days without any food at all. Each day, I found myself tightening my belt one more notch, just like a cartoon wolf.

When I finally managed to get food stamps, life got a little easier for me. I was able to eat more frequently, and though it wasn't much money for food, it was a lot more than what I'd had before. I didn't have to dig through the trash anymore, so I was able to focus more effort on finding work. Still feeling a bit uneasy about having them, I used the EBT benefit only when I needed to. On weeks where I could sustain myself on the income I earned, I wouldn't use my EBT card. I did eventually manage to elevate my life to a point where I didn't need the food stamp benefit at all. I felt really good about that because to me, I was a little more independent. It made me feel normal. However, working as a freelancer provides much less of a guarantee of income than having a typical job. For all of 2017, I have not been able to provide for myself, but thank the Lord that I have been in places where that doesn't have as much of an impact as it typically would. Actually, I have lived in two different places in 2017, so far. They both have their pros and cons. For instance, in the first place I was living, I didn't have to pay for anything really. Even my cell phone bill was being taken care of. However, the actual living conditions were incredibly stressful for me. The second place, where I am presently living as I write this guide, is a lot less stressful in many ways, but I am responsible for my own bills. So, I have to find ways to make enough money to pay for my cell phone each month. I also have other occasional bills that pop up as well, not to mention a mile-high pile of debt that is capitalizing on me. Though I've said it once, I'll say it again, it sure beats sleeping on the street.

If you're familiar with the northern Midwest region of the United States, you are aware that winter and early spring are very bitterly cold times of year there. For a time in my life, which I hope never to have to repeat, I spent a week or so living on the street during early spring. What more, I didn't have warm clothes on. I didn't have any money. I didn't have, really, anything. I managed to find a nice warm place to stay for two of the nights, but for the rest of the time, it was me against the elements. I was scared that it was the end for me, and I was incredibly hungry. After a few days, I also became ill. I begged and pleaded with God to deliver me from that awful experience. As sure as I am telling you the story now, he did. Again, that is something I describe in my memoir, Dear Baby: Letters To A Child Who Was Never Mine. I bring it up here is because there are many other people living out on the street who don't make it through the bitter cold of winter. They freeze to death out on the street. Granted, many people lose the ability to think clearly when they come face to face with their demise.

I, on the other hand, become highly alert. My brain switches to survival mode and I focus on nothing else but making it through to another day. I moved about very slowly to avoid breaking a sweat because I knew it would increase my chances of hypothermia. It would also cause me to smell bad, which would make me stand out more. I wanted to fit in because it meant being able to do "normal people" things like slipping into a restaurant to use their restroom and grabbing a cup of water on the way out. If there was nobody else in the restroom with me, I'd freshen up as much as I could to keep odors down. I managed to eat for two of the days but otherwise stayed away from digging through the trash for scraps, as so many other homeless people do. I have a thing about sharing food and drink as it is, and I knew that eating food from the trash could seriously endanger my life. Although, even if food poisoning didn't get me, there was a great chance that the bitter cold would have.

How Poverty Effects My Life

I've shared much detail regarding what poverty looks like for me, a natural-born American. Poverty doesn't care who you are, nor where you come from. Any notion that a person who is born in America is somehow better off than someone born outside of America is total nonsense. In fact, I know plenty of folks in foreign countries whose lives are much better than mine. They can afford to put a roof over their heads, food on their tables, clothes on their backs. Yet, poverty erodes their countries too, just as it does America. In this final section of chapter one, I'll describe how poverty effects my life. You're probably thinking that this seems redundant, but I'm not referring to the surface-level stuff. I'm referring to the longterm consequences it has had on my life and the ways that it has changed me. There are numerous consequences poverty has had on my life. Some of these are good, while others bad. I will describe some of these consequences in this section, in no particular order. The first consequence I'd like to discuss regards my worldview. The longer I've lived in poverty, the less important being an American seems to be, and the more important being a child of God has become. This change comes as a result of realizing that every time I've opened my eyes to a new day, it's not because America loves me or cares anything about me, it's because the Lord loves me and cares everything about me. I've rebounded from the deepest depths in my struggle with poverty, not because America has rescued me, but because God has come looking for me. At one point in time, I would have told you that being an American was just as important to me as being a child of God, but time has revealed that isn't the case anymore. Being a child of God is much more important to me, and being an American is no longer of much significance at all. In the past, I was an American concerned about the wellbeing of other Americans. Now, I am a person concerned about the wellbeing of other people. My heart goes out to the lowly and suffering, regardless of whether or not they come from the same country as me. There was a time when I, like so many other people, used the word love sparingly. Love was something that a person had to go above and beyond to earn from. Even in my struggles, God has never made me earn his love and, likewise, doesn't expect that I should make anybody earn love from me either. So, my love is given more freely now. I love people first and foremost, it's liking them that takes some work. All things considered, it's as if poverty has turned me into a mirrored image of who

I once was. Surely, by now there are readers who are scoffing at me, probably calling me some choice names, and putting words into my mouth concerning my stance on political and economic affairs in America, and all because I've indicated that being an American isn't as important to me as being a child of God. Ironically, some of these people profess to be devout in their faith as well, yet now hurl insults at me because of mine. For the sake of edification, I would like to say that I avoid politics as much as I can because the average modern politician is a self-involved, greedy liar primarily concerned with funding their own retirement.

Another long-term effect that living in poverty has had on me involves a magnification of reality. That magnification has multiple consequential facets to it, and one of them is an inability to manifest a phony positive attitude, which seems to be a popular thing to do these days. I have seen so many cliche motivational quotes circulating on social media in recent years that I want to cry. They're all just so ridiculous and most of them are nothing more than rephrased versions of other ridiculous motivational quotes created by somebody needing validation. And what do any of these quotes do besides mislead people into believing in unrealistic goals and setting unrealistic expectations for life? I truly hope that once people run out of these nonsensical quotes, they have something of greater substance to hang their hope on. You may think me pessimistic, but the word you should be searching for is realistic. There is failure in life, a lot of it. Trying to avoid it is futile and denying it is a senseless waste of a valuable lesson. It's not the actual failing that a person should be worried about anyhow, it's how they respond to it that matters. Realistically, I know that the American Dream is nothing more than a lottery, and just as I don't spend too much time playing the lottery, I don't put too much effort into hanging onto the American Dream (hence the carefully, yet creative, title I came up with for this series). However, that doesn't mean I don't dream. In fact, another of the facets is that my dreams and imagination are better defined and more lucid than ever. You didn't misread that, having a better understanding of reality has enabled me to dream better and imagine more. The third facet that's occurred as a result of reality being magnified is how I set expectations of people I encounter on a daily basis. As most of us are well aware, people tend to fail us, and sometimes it's in very big ways. At one point in my life, every time a person let me down it felt like a knife going through my heart. However, now I almost come to expect it. That is, whenever I'm actually foolish enough to put my hope in another person. I am not saying that there isn't anybody who can be depended upon, but I find that those people are brought into my path when I trust in God and not people. For me, living in a world of reality has been of much more use than living in a world of positivity. Although, the two terms are not exclusive, even though it seems that they are regarded as such. I am still very positive, but it is realistic positivity that has realistic expectations.

The final long-term effect that I want to talk about in this section relates to how poverty has robbed me of time. The most valuable resource that any of us has is time. We are born into this world with a finite amount of it. We cannot get any more than our finite amount, but what makes time such a terrifying topic for many people is that there is no indication of when that finite amount of such a precious resource will expire. That is why we ought to make the most out of what time we do have. For someone living in poverty, however, the amount of control they have over what they do with their time is greatly hindered. Poverty demands attention and most of my time the past several years has been focused on getting it out of my life. I have missed so many memories with my family on the holidays. I have given up time spent with people who meant the world to me, but who are no longer here in the world with me. And now, though I do try not to dwell on it, I sometimes lay awake and wonder how my life would have been different if not for poverty. I imagine the memories I could have been part of and the wisdom I could have obtained from those who have departed from this place. The phony motivational quotes would have me believe that I need to pay no mind to the time I've lost, that I need to focus on the time I have left. However, the reality is that while poverty continues to plague my life, I remain a prisoner of it. And the longer I remain a prisoner of poverty, the more accomplishments and experiences I miss out on. Just as anybody else doesn't, I do not know when my time here is up. It could be at any moment, but when I look back on the moments that have already passed I can say that I am underwhelmed by what I have accomplished in my life. Then again, that's what most prisoners do, and poverty is truly a daunting prison sentence. All I can do is continue serving that sentence within the boundaries that it creates until the time comes when I am truly free and can begin to live my life. I await that day and am hopeful for it. While I wait, I remain steadfast in prayer that it should come sooner than later. I have shared ways poverty has had longterm effects on my life. It is by no means an exhaustive list of consequences, as there have also been effects on my health as well, but I hope that you have a clearer understanding of the long reach poverty has on a person, even an American. And though I have been able to share some of my story with you through this guide, there are many more suffering in poverty who don't have such a platform but who are suffering nonetheless.

CHAPTER TWO
Poverty Statistics for The Land of Opportunity

Poverty in America

Now that you've heard how poverty affects my life, we'll look at the bigger picture, how poverty effects Americans. Before doing that, though, we'll look at some statistics regarding poverty's presence in America. I'm not the only one who suffers from poverty. Actually, it is quite a widespread issue here in the "Land of Opportunity." As I've said before, poverty doesn't care who you are or what your background is. It doesn't care what your race or ethnicity is, whether white or black, Hispanic, Asian or otherwise. It also doesn't care if you're educated or not because there are both educated and uneducated individuals living in poverty in America. In fact, I have a Bachelor's degree, am working on a Master's degree, and yet, I live in poverty. Gender and age also don't affect poverty's spread. There are males and females of all ages who suffer from the pangs of poverty, from children all the way up to senior citizens. But what determines who is and is not considered impoverished? In the United States, the Federal government sets a threshold that determines what the poverty level is. The poverty threshold, as it's called, fluctuates annually and is based on data compiled by the Census Bureau. The latest published data, from 2016, is available from the bureau in the form of a spreadsheet. One can easily deduce that the threshold varies based on family size and the number of children under the age of 18. It is also worth noting, the US Census Bureau indicates that the threshold is a weighted average. With that in mind, the threshold, or weighted average threshold, for a single person without any children is $12,228 annually. As low as that number is, there are Americans, such as myself, who fall below it. As of present, I haven't earned even $10,000 this year and am struggling to come up with $80 each month to pay my cell phone bill with. What's really sad is that there are many other Americans in my same position, some of them are even worse off. As you'll see in the following section, I've provided data from The Salvation Army USA, which illustrates a breakdown of particular groups of people who are heavily impacted by poverty here in America. Those groups include children, disabled people, senior citizens, and veterans. Of course, these aren't the only groups of people who are dealing with poverty. I'm not a child, nor disabled, nor a senior citizen, and I am not a combat veteran. However, I am still struggling with poverty. The demographics covered in the data from The Salvation Army USA only include the groups of people that tend to get the most attention in this country. In addition to those listed, you could add women. And when you really want to draw attention to your case, you can add an ethnicity or skin color. Without going into any great detail, I'll say that Caucasian or white isn't among those commonly used. We'll leave it at that because I risk a lot of backlash for even mentioning such a fact. For the record, the groups mentioned tend to be considered most vulnerable, but as I continue to repeat, poverty doesn't care who are or what your background is. It doesn't care what your race or ethnicity is, whether white or black, Hispanic, Asian or otherwise. It doesn't care if you're educated or not. And, just as equally noteworthy, it doesn't care what your gender is. As redundant as I might be, repeating that over and over again, I can't actually stress those facts enough. Poverty can and does affect anybody. However, it seems that only certain groups of people, or demographics, are getting any attention.

Not only is poverty unconstrained by who it effects, the manner in which it affects them is not limited either. Two of the more common consequences of poverty are homelessness and hunger. Though, there are people who are just barely able to afford to keep a roof over their heads and food on the table who are still impoverished. If you'll recall, my parents managed to keep our family sheltered and fed, but there isn't much else we could afford. That's why we were so grateful when people from our church would send over bags of hand-me-down clothes. It doesn't matter if you drive through urban or rural America, you'll see the signs of poverty's hold on the nation. In urban America, you'd see homeless people throughout major cities. They sometimes create tent communities near abandoned buildings and under overpasses. If you go by soup kitchens and shelters, you'll see long lines of people who have no other means of sustaining themselves. In rural America, you'll find communities of mobile homes and trailers. These dwellings tend to cost a lot less than a traditional stick-built house, which is why they pop up so frequently in areas of rural America, where the cost of living tends to be much lower. In terms of eating, impoverished people tend to have diets that are not as well balanced and nutritious as people who are not. Even those impoverished people utilizing some sort of government food supplement program tend to not eat as healthy as they should. As important as maintaining a healthy diet is, doing so is an expensive undertaking for any American. That fact is entirely ironic, but it is true nonetheless. Most of the essentially important things we need are pricey, though. Things like a healthy diet, decent health insurance, visits to the doctor, medicine, and even the cost of hygiene products and other toiletries. Most people living in poverty are faced with having to choose which of these things they want to spend their money on, choosing between purchasing medicine or putting food on the table. It becomes a vicious cycle that further decreases that person's quality of life. I hadn't realized just how serious it was until the first time I ever received food stamps. I went to the grocery store needing food, but also needing toothpaste and shampoo. When I went to purchase the items, I was shocked that my food stamps couldn't be used for the toothpaste or shampoo. However, they would allow me to purchase junk food, candy, and other stuff I didn't actually need to survive. Granted, it is a *food* supplemental program, but hygiene products are just as equally important to one's survival as food products are. It seems that, perhaps, the food supplemental programs administered by the government need to reconsider what can and cannot be purchased with program benefits. Then again, the government is a major part of the reason why poverty is so rampant in America.

One of the most common questions asked amid a major problem like poverty is why. Why is this happening? In the case of poverty, the American government is largely to blame. There are many theories and opinions regarding this. Some would suggest it's a certain political party's fault, while others would suggest that it is because of the economic system we have in place here. I think that most of the theories and opinions are biased, and are created by people who don't actually have a clear understanding of the problem because they don't have firsthand experience with the problem. When I say that the problem is largely the fault of the government, I am not pointing fingers at one political party or the other, nor am I pointing fingers at America's capitalism-based economy. I am pointing fingers at the American government collectively, which is primarily run by greedy, incompetent individuals who don't know what poverty actually looks like, and quite frankly, they probably don't care either. I will go into much more depth on this in the next chapter when I provide my commentary on the problem of poverty in America, but for now, I will say that the root of the problem is greed and arrogance, both of which stem from the government. That said, Americans continue to fall for the empty promises of political candidates and continue to vote for them. The only people becoming less impoverished, better sheltered, better fed, better insured, and better off altogether are the elected politicians themselves. All the while, a notable percentage of the American population continues to struggle just to make ends meet. To that end, I suppose it might be said that Americans have more in common with Romanians than we might think. For Romanians, though, it was a single madman who drove their economy into the ground. For Americans, it is an oversized and overpaid system of greedy, self-concerned politicians known as the Federal government.

Poverty by The Numbers

In the case of poverty in America, the numbers are truly shocking when compared to the idealized reputation this nation has around the world. According to statistics reported by several organizations focused on poverty in America, there are roughly 40 million Americans living in poverty. And based on a 2016 US population statistic of 324,872,750, that means 1 out of every 8 Americans is living in poverty. If the United States is supposed to be a land of opportunity, this is a terrifying truth! The reality hits a little closer to home when you look a bit closer at the breakdown from The Salvation Army USA:

- **20%** of children under the age of 18 are living in poverty.
- **8%** of seniors age 65 and older are living in poverty.
- **29%** of those living with disability are living in poverty.
- **6%** of America's veterans are living in poverty.

Being a nation that constantly boasts its patriotism, that constantly talks about the gratitude it has for those who've defended it as soldiers and first responders, the number of veterans living in poverty in America should be zero! However, that is not the case. Moreover, as a nation that professes to be a place for dreamers, we have a disturbingly high number of children who suffer in poverty each day. On their website, The Salvation Army USA really puts it into perspective, "Among the 35 wealthiest countries in the world, the United States has the second-highest child poverty rate! One out of every five children lives below the poverty line." Perhaps these truths haven't dawned on you until now, or maybe you just don't understand what the big deal is. Can't these people just get jobs? It isn't so simple. Poverty is truly a plague that creates a chaotic imbalance across various aspects of a person's life. As someone who is suffering from poverty, I can attest to these things. The whole reason I advocate for the impoverished is because I know what they're going through. Poverty doesn't just mean not having a lot of money and nice things, it means not having enough money to minimally get by, put a roof over one's own head, put food on the table. It also typically means not having readily available access to resources necessary to turn things around for themselves (I.e., phone, Internet). Yes, poverty is simply the vicious root of numerous painful symptoms.

For the remainder of this section, we will look more into each demographic highlighted in the breakdown above. And because America presents itself as a nation of patriots who truly value those who've served it, we'll start with veterans. According to the Bureau of Labor Statistics, a division of the US Department of Labor, roughly 453,000 veterans were unemployed in 2016. That number has decreased nearly 21% since a similar report was released back 2015 with the findings of the prior year's data. That report indicates 573,000 veterans were unemployed in 2014. Despite the overall decrease in veteran unemployment, the number of veterans living below the poverty threshold is still disturbing. A report from the US Department of

Veteran Affairs dated May 2015 indicates that "...the veteran poverty rate is rising." The report demonstrates that the percentage of veterans living below the poverty threshold has increased 8.7% between the reporting periods of 2005-2007 and 2010-2012. While that might not seem like a very big increase, you must recall that these statistics consider veteran poverty on a national level. So, in other words, the report indicates that the number of veterans living below the poverty threshold in the 2005-2007 reporting period, which was 1,348,794, increased 8.7% in the 2010-2012 reporting period to a new total of 1,465,807 veterans living below the poverty threshold. Increased efforts from private and non-profit organizations, such as the United States Veteran Initiative, have been making a positive difference for America's veterans. On their website, this organization professes to assist veterans with securing permanent and transitional housing, jobs, and even provides counseling and family services. Unfortunately, a number of similar organizations exist that also profess to aid veterans, but actually use funds for frivolous purposes. One such organization, Wounded Warrior Project, only spends 60% of its budget on assisting veterans, according to a March 2016 report from CBS News. The Federal government should be doing something to thwart organizations like this, which can ultimately help in decreasing the number of American veterans living in poverty.

Another disturbing demographic is the number of senior citizens living in poverty. These are folks who worked a majority of their lives contributing to a nation that promised to care for them once they retired. However, too many of these hard-working citizens have been left to fend for themselves, some having to come out of retirement to provide for themselves and their dependent family members. The National Council on Aging (NCOA) reports that "Over 25 million Americans aged 60+ are economically insecure—living at or below 250% of the federal poverty level..." Ironically, even Social Security cannot remedy this. In a radio address on the third anniversary of the Social Security program in America, then President Franklin Roosevelt touted, "... this system is designed to assure them an income for life after old age retires them from their jobs." Yet, the failing system still leaves America's elderly with soaring medical costs to struggle with, in addition to basic living expenditures. The official poverty rate generally includes income from government programs like Social Security, which means that seniors collecting this benefit wouldn't get counted as being impoverished. However, the rate without Social Security would have been around 24.4% in 2011, a notable difference from the reported 16.1%, according to May 2013 article from The Washington Post. The article goes on to explain why that statistic isn't as good for seniors as it might seem at first glance:

> *While the SPM takes transfer payments into account, it does the same with out-of-pocket medical costs. If you're an unmarried senior with no dependents, make $15,000 a year, and spend $10,000 of it on medical care, under the official poerty measure you'd most likely not count as poor, as $15,000 is above the 2012 poverty threshold for a single senior ($11,011).*

This is a great example of how statistics can be carefully swayed to communicate whatever the person calculating them wants them to communicate, and the Federal government in America certainly doesn't want to demonstrate that its senior citizens are getting shorted in their retirement. Meanwhile, these elderly parents and grandparents are suffering, many being forced out of their own homes. The NCOA reports that "Approximately 3.5 million older homeowners are underwater on their loans and have no home equity."

So, in addition to those who've served America in the military, those who've worked hard and paid for its prosperity, who have been promised some level of security in their retirement, are left struggling by a nation who would rather focus its attention on an ego that it can't rightly defend anyhow.

Finally, I'll combine the last two demographics because children and the disabled are both demographics of people who are reliant upon aid from able-bodied family members and/or government programs. Ironically, they are also the two demographics with the highest percentage living in poverty. According to the breakdown from The Salvation Army USA, children and the disabled account for nearly half of the impoverished in America. There is something to be said about a nation who boasts the largest economy in the world, yet who also has the highest relative rate of child poverty. According to the Children's Defense Fund, a private nonprofit organization, "America ranks 34th in relative child poverty—ahead only of Romania whose economy is 99 percent smaller than ours." To put it in other words, 1 in every 7 children will be born into poverty in the United States." The total sum of impoverished American children, based on my research, seems to be right around 15 million. America's disabled people are in a similar situation, maybe slightly worse if you agree with the notion that "Disability is both a cause and consequence of poverty." An article appearing on NPR's website states that "Fewer than 1 in 5 disabled adults are employed, one reason so many are poor." It's worth noting that among these disabled individuals are many of America's veterans. As we've already discussed, that is a demographic that already suffers much more than it should, but now we see that it is overlapped by another demographic that only adds to the overall need for action. Switching back to children, I can't help but think of the large number of organizations that exist to fight childhood poverty and hunger, and there are literally hundreds and hundreds of organizations that focus on this mission. Yet, the statistics demonstrate that the level of childhood poverty in America is still high enough to rank it adjacent to Romania, a country that is living with the consequences of many years under a terrible and greedy ruler. America cannot use that same excuse, even though it has seen its share of under-qualified presidents and other politicians. Moreover, America's economy dwarfs that of Romania by a lot. The quote from the Children's Defense Fund indicates that America's economy is 99% larger than Romania's, yet somehow poverty is just as widespread here as it is there.

By reviewing the statistics provided in this section, one should be able to identify that America is clearly suffering from the pangs of poverty. Although, I hope you won't simply take my word for it. As you should have seen at the bottom of each page, I've included footnotes for all of my research, and there are plenty of additional resources available related to the topic of poverty in America. The additional effort will only help you better understand the extent to which poverty plagues the "Land of Opportunity."

The Cost of Poverty in America

Americans often go about their day-to-day lives never putting much thought into the fact that poverty in America actually has negative impacts on their lives as well. In this section, we will look at how America's poverty problem is actually a problem for those who aren't even living in poverty just as much as it is for those who are.

You might be utterly bewildered by the notion that someone not living in poverty could be just as impacted by it as someone who is living in poverty. However, it is true, and poverty costs American taxpayers billions and billions of dollars annually. Childhood poverty, particularly, is said to account for a majority of it. An article about the costs of poverty published by the

Center for American Progress does a great job of explaining how this is possible. There are three main points the article makes. The first is concerned with health care. Because they tend to have poor diets when they are young, impoverished children tend to have poor health later in life. This creates major health care expenditures, which are paid for by tax dollars. It can also result in an earlier mortality, which means a smaller contribution to the economy. The second point made by the article involves a widely debatable statistic, that children who grow up in poverty are more likely to take part in criminal activity when they are older. This can result in huge costs within the criminal justice system, which are also paid for with tax dollars. The third point the article makes considers an impoverished child's overall ability to contribute to the economy over the course of their life. Since they are said to have poorer health, they also tend to have poorer and lesser productivity. In other words, they take from the economy more than they give to it. As you can see, there are numerous variables at play. After all, as we've seen, poverty is actually a lot more than just not having enough money or resources. There are many other facets to the problem, that is, consequences that arise as a result of it. Now, although the excerpt details how childhood poverty impacts the American economy, some of the consequences are just as true of poverty plaguing any other demographic. For instance, senior citizens, veterans, and disabled people all tend to require more health care than the average individual. Since poverty means that these individuals cannot afford to pay the associated costs themselves, they are usually paid for by government-run social programs. These programs are funded by tax dollars, and the heavier the demand that's put on government-run social programs, the more tax dollars that must be collected in order to properly fund them.

All of these various costs on the economy and missed contributions back to it add up in a very big way. According to a September 2012 article appearing on Forbes' website, poverty costs American taxpayers roughly $550 billion annually. The writer of that article, Tim Worstall, poses a very logical question when he asks how America can still be in poverty when it spends so much on the issue. Surely he must have asked the question with some sense of irony because spending any amount of money on a problem does not ensure its resolution. It is how that money is being spent that can determine whether or not the problem will see improvement. In this case, the money isn't being spent on fixing the problem, but rather on poorly bandaging it. A report from The Heritage Foundation states that government spending on social programs has increased 16 times over since Johnson's war on poverty began, but little to no improvement has been seen of America's poverty problem, and that figure does account for inflation. Moving on, there is one more point concerning the cost of poverty in America that is worth having a look at.

Before sharing it with you, I want to say, once again, that it is truly a moot point. Yes, there is a lot of research that points to this issue as being a contributing factor to how much poverty costs America, but that research seems to be inconclusive. I am, of course, referring to the notion that people who grow up in poverty or live in it for a sustained duration of time tend to engage in criminal activity. The logic behind this theory is that impoverished people, out of desperation or need, are more likely to commit crimes in order to elevate their circumstances. This, in turn, results in administrative costs within the criminal justice system, which is a further burden on American tax payers. It also results in major financial burdens on their victim(s). The problem with this theory, though, is that it tends to stereotype all impoverished people as being criminals. For as many people living in poverty who are committing crimes, there are just as many who are not committing crimes. So, though the logic behind the theory tends to make sense, there just doesn't seem to be a definitive way to link a person's impoverished status with their tendency to commit the crime. However, if there were a way, that would add an entirely new level to the cost of poverty in America. After all, estimates indicate that roughly 47% of all Americans live in poverty to some degree. Yet, even though there is no solid evidence supporting a direct correlation between poverty and crime, there is a correlation between crime and poverty. This is a more substantiated theory, and one whose findings ought to be factored into the cost of poverty in any nation. A December 2014 article published on Psychology Today's website elaborates on this theory. In the article, Dr. Stanton E. Samenow points to numerous cities in urban America, like Washington, DC and Ferguson, Missouri, in which civil unrest has resulted in a decline in the performance and presence of small businesses. When civil unrest results in the vandalism of and/or theft from small businesses, entrepreneurs are faced with great losses, including money, time, customers, sales, and even employees. Such an event can set off a chain of consequences that ultimately results in the entrepreneur being unable to re-open their business and a loss of income for them, as well as for their employees. And because of occurrences like these, new entrepreneurs avoid opening businesses in the affected area out of fear that they will be met with the same catastrophes. While it might not be advantageous to conclude that poverty causes crime, it seems safe to say that crime causes poverty. And consider this, when crime forces a fledgling entrepreneur out of business and into poverty, they are likely to enroll in one or more government-run social programs, which in turn increases the financial burden on the American taxpayer and widens the spread of poverty as taxes increase to satisfy the higher demand on said programs. Though there is a lot more that could be said about how America is spending money on poverty, such a discussion is better suited for the following section, in which I provide extensive commentary. Afterward, I will wrap up this guide by offering some solutions that could viable improve America's poverty problem.

CHAPTER THREE
Commentary and Solutions

My Commentary on Poverty in America

America: The Land of Opportunity; America: Land of The Free and Home of The Brave; America: Give Us Your Tired, Your Poor, Your Huddled Masses Yearning to Breathe Free. Over the years, many titles and phrases have emerged, which cause one to believe there is truly some unique paradise to be discovered within these borders. However, this land is not much different from any other, at least, not anymore. It's not to say that these slogans, and that's exactly what they are, were not justifiable at one point in time. However, America has changed dramatically since then. We have problems here just as any other country does. We've got greed, scandal, murder, theft, terrorist attacks, you name it. We've also got plenty of politicians who do their damnedest to further the destruction of this once great nation. And, in case you've been led to believe otherwise, we've got poverty, homelessness, and hunger, and a lot of it too. For all of the commotion we've been experiencing over immigration here the past several years, I cannot understand why. Why so many people are so bent on coming to this place, that is. The only viable answer I have been able to come up with is that they've been given false information. Somehow, they've been led to believe that America is a wonderful place, full of opportunity and prosperity. That it is a place of freedom. If you're reading this, and it's you I've just described, I hate to be the bearer of bad news but I've lived here my entire life and the majority of that stuff isn't true anymore. So, if you've been planning on relocating to America in search of a better life, which I'm sure has taken a lot of hard work and effort, I suggest you stop and think about what you're doing. In reality, this place is probably not much better than where you are now, just different. Now, I'll admit, that might not be the case for all of you, but I'd dare say it is for most of you. I would strongly caution you to reconsider coming here if it's poverty, homelessness, or hunger you're seeking to escape because, as I've said, we've got plenty of that here. America is an expensive place to live, and if you can't afford it, this place will eat you up alive and spit out the bones. Yes, I can tell you from experience that this nation is very cold and unforgiving, especially to the impoverished and lowly. There are social programs and other resources available to help those struggling make ends meet, but those programs are intended to provide minimal help. And there are so many people dependent on those programs and resources, they're always in short supply. What's more, the average American taxpayer has grown weary of paying such high taxes to keep these programs sufficiently funded, and in all honesty, they should be able to keep more of their hard earned money for themselves. Though I live in poverty, I don't believe that anybody should be forced by the government to pay for me to thrive. That said, I do think there are moral, ethical, and religious arguments to be made about people helping their fellow man when they've got abundant resources with which to do so, but I will save that all for a bit later. The bottom line at this point, America isn't the paradise you might believe it is. For the duration of this section, I will provide commentary on one of America's most prevalent, yet seemingly most ignored problems, poverty. If you're an American who easily gets offended when someone says things about America that don't present it as being a flawless and magical land, I suggest you stop reading at this point. Why? I'm not a nationalist and don't believe in touting any country to be more than it actually is. These are my thoughts, which are based on my experiences.

My Commentary on Poverty in America

Up to this point, I've attempted to define what poverty in America is by illustrating it for you using my own personal experiences. Afterward, I attempted to demonstrate that it's a much more widespread issue than most people realize and provided statistical data from relevant sources. Now, I will draw on all of that, personal experiences and data, to offer my own commentary. The major point I will touch upon is where, I believe, the poverty issue in America stems from. If I haven't already made my position abundantly clear, I believe that it is mostly the fault of its government. I am not sure I have to argue that all too much because modern history proves that anything involving government intervention is broken, inefficient, and incapable, and those are only a few of the words I could have chosen. Politics in America are more a sport than anything else. The players, politicians, get paid a lot of money to support their team by creating havoc for the opposing team, no matter the cost. That is how establishment politics works. At one point in time, being a politician wasn't a career choice. However, now it is, and it comes with a lot of perks. The hardest part of being a politician is getting your constituents to believe that you have their best interest in mind and are actually getting things accomplished, so they'll continue voting for you. The referees in this game are our judges, and they're willing to play dirty too. They get in through the dirty work done by the establishment they favor, and that puts them in a position to push their team's agenda on the nation while making things miserable for the opposing team. And this ego-driven power struggle goes back and forth on a daily basis because too many of America's citizens foolishly believe that their politician wants to help them and help this nation. The truth is, the politicians have failed us, and they continue to fail us each and every day. The modern politician is one of America's biggest problems and is at the very root of everything that plagues its citizens.

In 1964, President Lyndon B. Johnson gave his notorious State of the Union address in which he officially "declared war on poverty." Almost 54 years later, poverty remains a major issue for America. Though, it's just not as important a topic for most Americans anymore, despite its impact on the economy. On one hand, poverty hinders the economy. On the other hand, the economy aids in poverty's spread. And it's the politicians perpetuating it with their mismanagement of time, money, and the other resources available to them. Not only that, but they've changed what's important in the eyes of their constituents, or fans, by vilifying and bullying them into submitting to a new agenda. That new agenda focuses on one major mission, and that's tearing down the opponent with straw man attacks, scandals (some of which are falsely manufactured), and other senseless attacks that fail to address any of America's real problems. You may be asking yourself why they would want to do such a thing. That's a simple question which has a simple answer. Money and power. The only things an establishment politician is concerned with are money and power, and they will stop at nothing to get both. Meanwhile, this nation continues to suffer and lose its identity. Do you think that matters to most Americans? They'll tell you it does, but that is only because that's what their establishment cheerleaders have told them to say. Most Americans only care about America insofar that their team is winning in the political match. Most Americans are so focused on the match that they have scarcely a clue as to what this nation's real problems are or where they stem from. Most Americans vote purely based on their allegiance to a political establishment instead of whats best for the country, and neither track-records nor history play much of a role in their decisions. If that weren't the case, even fewer Americans would show up on election days, but that's not the case. Americans are voting these people into office!

That's one thing that the major political establishments seem to agree on, that voting is incredibly important. Well, of course it is because it's the only way they can continue their conquest for power and money. So, they all partake in the campaign to encourage voting, which involves bullying Americans into choosing a candidate or voting a certain way for a bill. You see, they've created a stigma out of not voting. If a person does not vote, they're not very American. If a person does not vote, then they're contributing to the problems America faces. Oddly enough, voting is the only right Americans have that is pushed as a requirement. You won't see any other right being pushed with as much vigor, including the right to keep and bear arms (aka. gun ownership). I haven't personally voted in many years now because I refuse to elect individuals who only seek to serve themselves, and I refuse to vote on bills that are primarily aimed at creating wealth and power for the establishments themselves. Many people have come out against me because of that choice. Some call me names, and others insist that I must vote because it's my right. I always respond the same way, by explaining that voting is a right, not a requirement. Some people attempt to rebut me at that point by indicating that if I don't vote, I can't complain about the outcome. I have a universal response to that notion as well. I explain that as long as I am an American citizen I will, in fact, complain about any American politician, law, or bill that opposes my ethical and/or moral points of view. If I don't like the candidates who are running, I am not going to go against my better judgment and vote for the sake of voting, and the same goes for bills. I refuse to be bullied into making choices I know ought not to be made, and if that makes me *un*-American, then so be it. In reality, it makes me more of an American than those who are voting "for the lesser of two evils," as they tend to put it.

What Can Be Done About Poverty in America?

Though I abstain from voting, I don't sit idly by and complain for the sake of complaining. I take clearly defined and well-supported stances against candidates and bills, and I vocalize those stances whenever I get the chance. That's why you're reading this book right now. As I have stated before, I believe that those who want to lament problems better also have solutions, or at least productive thoughts that could lead to solutions. Otherwise, just having an opinion for the sake of having one is a total waste of time, which roots itself in arrogance and ego. I certainly don't want to be viewed as one who spouts off baseless opinions, so I offer the following solutions to the problem of poverty in America. At first glance, I'm certain that many of you will question how they relate to poverty. Let me assure you that they do! As any good medical doctor would tell you, to conquer an illness you must treat the cause as well as the symptoms. My solutions, first and foremost, seek to tackle the root cause of the poverty issue. The good thing about that, the root cause of poverty is also the root cause of many other problems America faces. So, in essence, my solutions address multiple problems simultaneously. How efficient is *that*?

The very first thing that needs to happen, the fringe benefits and perks that come with being a career politician need to be dramatically reduced and lobbying needs to be strictly prohibited. By reducing the number of personal gains one can acquire through serving in a political position, representing the people becomes more of a task for those who are in it to genuinely serve without concern for personal gain. This seems like an obvious and necessary step for America, yet politicians are still able to "answer the call" of public service in an effort to afford posher lifestyles for themselves. And Americans continue to vote for these individuals, buying their empty promises of positive change. In reality, the only change there will be is the few cents those Americans are left with after the establishment fat cats get their fill. As I say that, it dawns on me that there may be readers who are unsure of what I mean when I refer to the establishment. Permit me a short digression and I will try my best to explain.

When American politics are being discussed on any real level, you will hear the term "establishment" thrown about. It refers to a coalition of individuals and organizations who control political power or authority. America uses a party system, so there are two major establishments, the Republicans, and the Democrats. They have deep roots in the political history of the nation, maybe too deep. An individual's ability to rise up in the ranks of one of these establishments depends largely upon their loyalty to it and their time in its ranks. This is commonly referred to as a "good ol' boy" system and is very cliquish. To put it all in terms I feel more people will understand, America's politics are led by two major aristocracies who are at war with one another to become America's dictatorship. And to keep American citizens from starting a literal war, those citizens are able to choose the individuals who will become their overlords from a selection of candidates the establishments have hand selected. This is what is referred to as the "right to vote." The candidates are those individuals, typically attorneys, since they're so accustomed to distorting the truth, who the establishment feels will best assimilate to its will, while also appealing to the people just enough to garner votes and support. As crazy as it sounds, this is how politics work in America, and how the establishment controls them. It's precisely why more and more citizens are speaking out against the establishment.

With that new understanding, and with the first solution having been already explained, let's continue on to my second solution. We've discussed how to make serving as a political figure just that, a service to the people and not a means to acquire wealth and power. The second solution to America's poverty problem, as well as a majority of its other problems, is eliminating all unnecessary and unconstitutional government spending. Since the forefathers first mapped out the Federal government back in 1787, it has expanded substantially, adding additional departments and agencies that increase operating costs, but that are also not necessary elements of the government. So why do they even exist? A dramatic expansion of the government is associated with former President Franklin D. Roosevelt's "New Deal," the government's attempt to counter the Great Depression. Part of that "deal" was the creation of 37 agencies, which were created in an to spark employment opportunities that didn't otherwise exist. However, what really came with the creation of these agencies was a larger government requiring a lot more money to operate. It was a terrible idea that seemed great at first, given the circumstances of the economy. In the long run, it has cost Americans a lot. Since then, many of these agencies have been dissolved, while some were merged into other agencies. Some of those which were dissolved met that fate after being deemed unconstitutional. That said, there are some that still exist, as well as other agencies that weren't part of the "New Deal" that could be eliminated or merged with other existing agencies to greatly decrease the size and operating costs of the government. This solution comes off as awfully obvious and elementary to me. If the operating costs of the government are greatly decreased, there will be a decrease in taxation. Americans will get to keep a lot more of the money they earn to improve their living conditions with. What's more, the tax monies the government is collecting can be more effectively utilized to tackle the national debt, which is incredibly out-of-hand and is the result of an oversized, mismanaged Federal government. One final note, and this point lends itself to a necessity for downsizing the Federal government and limiting its costs, many of the agencies have grown into oversized, mismanaged bodies within their parent oversized, mismanaged body. In other words, they have become their own governments within the government. "Trimming the fat" is, therefore, essential to effectively addressing problems, such as poverty.

Another solution, which addresses poverty a bit more head-on, involves lawmakers reviewing laws and regulations regarding non-profit/charitable organizations. More needs to be done to keep these organizations honest to their mission. The minimum amount of their budget spent on their particular cause(s) must be raised much higher, and there needs to be stricter monitoring of their annual budgets and various expenditures. Organizations which truly wish to make a positive change in the lives of the less fortunate need to be rewarded for their efforts by removal of hindrances that slow or stop them from carrying out their mission. On the other hand, organizations who profess to serve others but actually serve their executives and their own interests must be recategorized as for-profit organizations. After all, if they are operating like a for-profit organization then they ought not to have the perks and benefits of a non-profit organization. It's not to say that non-profit organizations shouldn't be able to pay their executives, management, and staff a livable wage. However, there are too many non-profit organizations that operate under false pretenses. They use their non-profit status, both, to fool people into making contributions and to keep more money by avoiding taxes on that income. The greatest amount of good done in this nation, in terms of poverty, homelessness, and hunger is done by non-profit charitable organizations. Much more than the government, they are familiar with the needs of people faced with these problems and they are doing a lot more to help them. In order to do that, they need to maintain necessary financial and other resources. So, in addition to the government removing any hindrances that would keep these organizations from doing so, it also needs to put measures in place that encourage people to continue donating generously and often. There is presently, as I write this, a tax measure being considered by Congress that would permit taxpayers the ability to claim charitable donations on their tax filing whether or not they itemize their deductions. As things stand, charitable deductions only benefit those people who choose to itemize their deductions and cannot be claimed by those who choose to take the standard deduction. Through this solution, America could see an increase in the effectiveness and efficiency of non-profit organizations that seek to help its less fortunate citizens.

Moving on to my next solution, and this one ties into the previous, the Federal government needs to restructure and possibly cut social programs it currently administers. In essence, the government would largely be stepping back from the charity role it plays, now that actual charities are in a position to carry out their respective missions much more effectively. Apart from providing services and aid to its veterans and elderly, the Federal government could and should cut way back on its social programming. Yes, I know that such a solution is bound to be met with sneers and grumbling, but the government is absolutely horrible at doing charity. It's been trying to do it for many years now, and consider the results. They are dismal. As I have already said, numerous times, private charitable organizations have been much more successful at reversing the effects of poverty on America than the government has. After all, a government is not a charity. It exists to govern and protect, and since one cannot use a knife as a spoon, perhaps its time to stop wasting so many resources on trying to do so.

The fifth and final solution I'm going to propose involves an old adage: "Give a man a fish and you feed him for a day; teach a man to fish and you feed him for a lifetime." We've discussed this before, but there is a false perception of America that causes people to believe that if they do not take care of themselves, the nation at large will be inclined to do so. This has resulted in much abuse of the social programs that currently exist, and that has greatly hindered the nation from moving forward in its recovery. Such abuse is yet another result of the government trying to behave as a charity. Such abusive activity needs to be swiftly ended. Those who have continually abused the system ought to be made to pay back that which they've stolen from the American people, either monetarily or by being given a high number of volunteer hours to fulfill with a local charity. Additionally, the aforementioned perception at the root of this all must be eliminated. America must focus on truly being the land of opportunity, as opposed to the land of ineffective welfare and handouts. There are many able-bodied people who could easily support themselves if their situation enabled them to do so. Numerous charities, such as The Salvation Army, place a heavy emphasis on skill development and job placement. Nearly everybody could be doing something to earn a sustainable income if given a chance to exceed. And while they are getting on their feet, they need someone to support them so that they don't end up falling back into the same hole they're climbing out of.

These solutions focus on cutting wasteful government spending, empowering charitable organizations to do what they do more effectively, and encouraging individuals to contribute to those organizations more often and generously, among other things. One cannot expect to undo years and years worth of damage with the implementation of four solutions but by taking small positive steps, such as these, greater momentum can be generated in the effort to end poverty in America, and to address numerous other problems that nation is faced with as well. I hope that this guide has given you a new perspective on life in America and on specifically how poverty affects it. I hope you will join me in volume 2 of The American Scheme when we'll take a look at the problem of homelessness in this nation.

MORE TITLES FROM

Jared A. Snyder

A true story about finding faith and the courage required to keep it in the face of adversity. In this thrilling memoir, author Jared A. Snyder explains how he became homeless after thwarting an abortion and provides transcriptions of the actual letters he penned in his journal to this child who was never really his, but who he fought for all the same.

eBook and Paperback

Made in United States
North Haven, CT
04 November 2026

21770208R00044